Published by Good Stuff Books

ISBN: 979-8-9944348-1-9
This book is a work of fiction. Names, characters, places, and incidents are either the product of the author's imagination or used fictitiously. Any resemblance to actual persons, living or dead, or actual events is purely coincidental.

Holy Ghosts and Hollywood Dreams

By
Jennifer Kain

Dedicated to the Dreamers
who won’t ever let those
bright lights
of the city
die

An Introduction of Sorts

Poetry told in three parts. While poetry is open to interpretation I must let you know that this collection is dedicated to the girl I was in my twenties. That unusual time in life where you're trying to pursue those dreams you've always had while also trying to pay rent for the first time, have your first adult job and try to date. These are the stories told through verse about those years.

This book is also dedicated to all those living life in Los Angeles right now who are in their twenties. This book is a love letter to my twenties.

So let's roll the scene.

Action..

In Order of Appearance

Part One

The Price of Hollywood Dreams

Dream Obsessed

What did I think would happen?
These professors filled in my
head,
with promises,
You can make it big
and it won't take time.

College fills your head with
nonsense,
hard work gets gold,
Fine, I'll take the bait,
let's see what I reel in.

For the love of a dream,
anyone believes.
It can be done,
You can win at life.
All you have to do is fly.

The cross-country drive takes
you,
to a land of cars, tar and
smoggy streets,
streets littered with trash,
comic books,
dumpster fires.
Cars honking,
people smoking,
endless lines,
theaters everywhere,
billboards for the latest
star budding,
this is the dream you say,
The path to stardom and
lights.

But first, the dead end job.
The job you hate just for the
dream,
sacrificing,
you love yourself that much,
It's worth obliterating
everthing else.
Who needs six when four or
three
hours will do.

The race to the top of the
Hollywood Hills
should be paved with the
tears of amateurs
all fighting
for that top spot.
Only work for free for a few
years,
relationship building is
gold.

Wash that guy's car,
and he will remember you
later,
when he's looking for an
assistant.
You go to dinner with old so
and so,
and you let his hand linger.
You don't get in his car
That's the one hard rule.

For the one true dream,
You might just have to be a
Lyft driver,
And wait it out.

Holy Ghosts And Hollywood Dreams

Neon lights blaze at Hollywood and Vine,
Mel’s Diner, a department store,
a man clutching a Bible sign,
shouting the world is going to Hell.

Buddy, I know that,
You don’t have to tell me twice,
I’m from the city of sin,
and moved to the city of Angels.

Here,
on Hollywood and Vine,
the crowds, stars, and wannabes,
Circus performers, Jack Sparrow impersonators,
All chasing a dream.

What is a dream?
except a promise,
reality can’t keep?

I came here with the best of
intentions,
but I left broken,
sad and confused,
At the timing of everything.

A time bomb, ticks, ticks,
ticks,
then stops.
Your time is up,
and you get sent out of the
club,

Was it worth it?
Holy ghosts drift down
Hollywood and Vine,
whispering through neon
light.
Your time is up.
Was it worth it?

Westsider

You, You, You, Who you are,
you Westsider, double-decker,
you who I know, we know,
why do I always have to visit
you?

Is the Westside entitled?
Are the streets paved with
gold?
There's usually no parking,
except if you live in one of
those,
unicorn, pony houses on a real
street,
not filled with apartments.

Oh Westsider, I know,
We live in neighborhoods in
the Valley,
there's parking in front of
our houses,
we have trees, and parks,
and houses that aren't a mil-
lion dollars.
Average folks live here.
And you can buy a house,
without selling a kidney.

Who are your neighbors?
Vacationers from Barcelona in
an Airbnb?
Taking selfies in front of
their manicured garden bed.
Yes, the beach, Santa Monica,
you're close,
We get it.

But California is more than
just the beaches,
Venice and Marina Del Rey,
Come see the valley.
We have hiking trails,
mountains,
and the Giving Tree.

You, you, you, Westsider,
one day, you will see.
Maybe you'll understand,
the glory of having space,
the joy of a car that can
actually fit in front of your
house,
the sweet, ordinary hum of
life.

Until then,
keep your golden streets,
and I will keep rebelling
against your
overpriced sand.

LA Hills

Off the 134 are hills,
Hills, hills, hills for days,
rolling and tipping
I imagine houses stacked on
top of another,
teetering like Dr.Seuss
sketches.

What if they were sideways?
Each leaning on their sides?

On a clear afternoon,
From the bend in the freeway,
downtown LA shimmers
through a pause in the smog.
The sprawl stretches,
green ridges,
suburbia and buildings,
houses upon houses,
sideways,
lopsided,
tilted
perfect in their imperfection.

But hills don't sit still,
One jolt,
one slip,
the ground beneath speaks,
quake, shake, shake.

Through binoculars,
is it the grey mediocrity you see?
After the glass shatters,
its song sings and streaks the sky,
Will it still stand alive?
The debris scatters the hillside.

From this hill
I can see all the way to 6th Street
a city balanced on a whimsy,
waiting for the ground
to cry,
to shriek,
to lurch,
to let go.

I Live on an Island

Anyone who questions me is a
liar,
I live on a landlocked island,
Surrounded by houses,
mountains,
The 134 and 5.

From the top of the hill
I look out as far as my eyes
can reach.
Still, I live on an island,
a place both seen
and unseen.

Quaint neighborhoods,
quiet as church mice,
What lurks behind
is only what you're meant to
know.

The windows are quiet,
full of the lives you want to
meet,
the artist, dreamer, lover,
and friend,
circulating,
living
that island dream.

Far from the traffic
the bubble lets you rest
Entering feels like a club
nobody knows about yet.

Burbank is my island
a city afloat in the valley,
adrift yet anchored,
forever apart,
forever its own
a secret you can almost see.

Just Pick Up the Phone

There's houses next to
apartments,
the urban sprawl,
A Barbie's pink shoe lies on
the ground,
A bag of old In-N-Out nearby.

A strung-out, bug-eyed man
passes,
staring as if I don't belong,
I keep my head down,
my pace quickens,
wishing I were a man,
not a lone woman walking,
back to my apartment at 11 pm.

I try to call you,
instead I talk to your stupid
voicemail,
at least then,
if I'm stolen away,
you'll know something
happened.

I hate the stares.
Everyone on this street,
sorry I’m the wrong color,
no, I don’t want your drugs,
or to be your friend.
Homegirl, Bae of drugged out
minions,
go stare elsewhere.

Don’t you know how it makes me
feel?
Go stare elsewhere,
Why doesn’t anyone,
Pickup their God damn,
Phone anymore?

No, I don't have Money, Sir

Cars. Cars. Stop. Stop.
Man, oh man, stop.
Playing music loudly. STOP.
For a moment of humanity.

Stop the music. Stop car.
Here, I'm here.
I'm here, notice me. Here.
Corner. Light. Red light.
Cars. Stop. Lights. Red.
Stop music. Stop light.

Signs. Stop. Music off.
Man. Stop. Lights stop.
Take me. Hear me. See me.
Help me, stop my sign,
Can I get sweet relief?
Sweet Jesus, stop.

Stop your car. Yellow light.
Stop and slow, man, oh man.
See me. Jesus, please see me.
I'm a man, and here's my empty
cup.
Please stop.

Stop, car. Man. Blink.
Push that pedal. Move.
Your sign. Off you
Go. Sad man eyes go.
Stop. Car. Blink eyes.

Green.

Disconnect

Hello.
Hi.
What's your name?
That's nice I'm Tom,
You play music?
I love music.
Coffee is life.
So is life.
Life is good with music.
I know right.
How do you get around town?
I don't drive?
You mean you've never tried?
No.
Ok.
I just don't have a car.
A thousand miles of
inconvenience.
Delete. Disengage.
Back away. Not my priority,
Disconnect.

A Dating Profile

Username: CoolBro85
25,
Writer, director, comedian,
Ask me what's the thing I'm
most likely to share:
Nothing! I'm an open book.
Must know The Name of the Wind
and quotes by Rick and Morty,
I love hiking, growing my
beard and
My cat. Here's me with my cat
Rupert.

Me: God forbid I don't know
every movie,
Me: You do,
You who loves to mansplain,
You who gets mad when I don't
get,
The pop culture joke you're
referencing.

Sorry too busy.
Too busy to see everything,
Too busy working to live,
The hustle is real, baby,
And hun, you're just going to
have to
Show me why ***[insert
pretentious film school movie
here]***
Is the greatest.
Because, darlin, I sure as
Hell don't care.

I went to film school, sure,
where every college student
had:
*Eternal Sunshine of the
Spotless Mind*,
Akira on their bookshelf, but
That does not make me a film
nerd
and a collector of every
shitty Criterion Collection
DVD.
Yes I said DVD because "In MY
DAY"
Blu Rays were still having the
debate with HD DVDs. Remember
those?
It's okay if you don't,
Blu Ray obviously won.

Next: Religion
Him: Agnostic with a slight bend towards Eastern religions involving Budha and the Taj Mahal
Love India.
Yeah and Curry.

Thanks for playing. NEXT.

www.okaycupid.com... Backup: Tinder. Bumble.
Let's see... Data loading zone... Feminist or follower? Loading. Loading. Loading.

A common interaction with a man online goes like this.

"I love Lord of the Rings too. What is visual effects? You're beautiful. Want to go get dinner?"
"Hi honey."
"Hi"
"Hey Beautiful"
"I don't care that I'm an atheist, I want to take you out and show you a good time."
"Girl you're pretty. Is religion really that important to you?"
"What do you mean you won't go on a date with me because I'm not a Christian?"
"Christian? Well, I mean, I grew up Catholic, doesn't that count?"

"That's fucked up. I can't believe you won't go out with me because I'm an atheist. I'm offended."
"I didn't know Christians were such bitches."
(Nobody called me a Bitch. But it got your attention, didn't it? I'm sure they thought it.)

See, here's my problem with online dating.
The man doesn't expect to get rejected once first contact is established and the girl responds. It's a shoe-in from there.
They expect that if they get a callback they've made it through the hardest part.
Now they just have to wine and dine her so they can get a cheap date out.

Am I wrong?

If I'm feeling lazy, I'll go on the date.
If I'm feeling like fighting, I'll say no
and explain why.

Here it goes.

Don't put me in your Christian
Girl Box.
Just because I say I want a
man who loves Jesus,
doesn't mean I don't love tacos, sex or having a good time
out.
What do you take me for, a
nun?

Him: Well, Girl, I frankly
don't understand why you won't
go on a date with me?
Me: You are not a Christian.
Simple as that.
You are hot and your pictures
make me want to kiss you,
but... wait that's too harsh.
I mean to say: I want to fuck
you in your pictures, but it's
only in my dreams. That will
never happen because you
aren't Christian.

Him: Can't we just coexist? It
works. My ex and I were
together for three years. And
we were different religions.

I think to counter him at this point:

WELL CLEARLY IT DIDN'T WORK.
Why do you think it will work this time round???
Him: Wow, what a fool. You're missing out.

NO BUDDY I'M NOT.
I WANT A MAN WHO APPRECIATES WHO I FUCKING AM.
AND BELIEVES JESUS IS THE COOLEST.

It's like people want tolerance, but just not for the other person.
What kind of noise is that?

Let me mansplain it to you this way, buddy.

Sorry, I don't fit into your perfect Christian Girl box.
The one who is kind, considerate, and oh so submissive to your every whim.

The man I marry will be of an
equal, and when I submit it’s
because we do it together. Not
the other way around, sir.

Move on, brother.
Block.

I Pray to the Spaghetti Monster

Dear God, I pray this date
will work,
Dear Spaghetti Monster, please
make my dreams come true,
Dear God, why did I give him
my number on the back of the
receipt?
Dear Spaghetti Monster, I
believe we have made a deal.

It was only one date,
one occurrence and I knew,
I could try it out.

That curly cue of golden
locks,
What a great night of ramen,
A face that could melt your
heart,
How are you so different?

Why did I have a type?
Or was I getting desperate?

What is it that you believe
in?
I believe in the Flying
Spaghetti Monster.

Heaven will be filled with
good tasting beer
and beautiful strippers.
The Spaghetti Monster gets me
out of work.
Religious occasions are
whenever I feel like it.

Wait. What's that now?
I don't think you're being
truthful here.

Is this a joke?
No, no, no.
You must be joking.

In New Zealand the Church of
the Flying Spaghetti Monster
lives.
One day when I die I will be
raised up to his land to meet
him.
I will then turn into a divine
being and live forever.

This is what I get for asking
someone out
In real life.

This Path

I didn’t think this night
would end this way.
I thought being in Silverlake,
where the hipsters lived,
Was the place to be on a
Saturday night.
In the hilly darkness,
I walked the orange, lighted
streets with this stranger,
Who was doing his best to
impress.

Did you know I already have
forgotten his face?
All I remember was eating
fancy hipster food,
And how I ended up with saliva
all over my cheek.

What is it about the way
someone acts to impress?
Should I have said no?
Should I have just took it?
What I did was,
was try and make the best of
it.

The alcohol in me did its
trick,
I was numb to it all.
It’s what I paid for:
this night, this guy,
this encounter.

Why did I let myself go?
How does straight liquor do
this to you,
mark you incapable of thinking
straight?
You only get this drunk
in the company of friends you
trust,
And family.

This occurrence should’ve been
the last time,
this path of a slobbering
mouth kissing my lips.
Did he fuck me?
I’m not too sure,
Sadly,
I don’t remember.

The fog of drinks, the late
night’s chill.
I remember only the Uber’s
arrival,
And the sheer relief.

A Change in Food

A culture of fried rice,
Ramen and tacos consumed me.
All I needed were these three.
It kept me warm and filled
when the conversation
started to die,
when I couldn't care one more
minute
about how the Marvel Cinematic
Universe fit together so
perfectly,
or why you loved bitter green
tea
So much.

I thought it was all so new
And exciting.
But I was wrong.
Now my soul has moved on,
filling my head with other
nonsense like ginger beers
and Moscow mules.

Who Am I?

Who am I?
What am I doing on Hollywood
Blvd?
Am I running errands?

Am I driving all day for the
man?
Getting groceries for the
group?
Wasting my time?

While my dreams fall farther
away?
What will become of those
dreams?
LA is what you make it.

Are you the next film
director?
Are you the next big shot?
Tell me really because
I don’t have time.

Where is your time?
is it flooded somewhere,
in a nonexistent dry channel?

Waiting for that water to
flow.
Only a few more jobs away.
And this time will be the big
time.
This time will be it.

Just keep waiting.
Waiting for my life to begin.
Why?
What makes you say that?

What were you meant to do?
What were you created to do?
Is it what you're doing right
now?

Who's God are you serving?

We all fall to our demons.

The question is,
What are you going to do about
it?

Part Two

My Body is a Ghost: Reruns

Destructive Love

Love is a bitter kind of
destruction,
When waiting,
Love is a red door to hatred,
It's a kind of false love that
sucks you in,
then spits you out, stung in a
place
no one wants to see.

The heart goes in thinking,
This time it will be
different,
He will feel this way, and
I'll give you all I got,
But it's always doomed.

In the end,
He will still die,
I will still mourn,
This cycle repeats,
Like a clock with no ending.

The corpse is fresh for
picking,
The idle hands keep an idle
watch for desire.
The mosquitoes suck the blood
until it's dry.

The heart wants what it knows
it should not.
Destructive love lasts for as
long
as the mind can handle,
Even after death, the heart
keeps thumping
through palindromes of saga.

Die to bitter truths,
To the love I once had.
Render me a corpse for loving
you.
We all fall into the gentle
Earth in the end.

The Feeling of You

The feeling of you,
the feeling of me,
the end of everything,
Trump is going to win,
No he isn't.

Laying on this lumpy air
mattress,
away from you,
the distance,
that ever-so-subtle space
means so much.
Why didn't I see it then?
We should've ended right there
and then.

His predictions were too
painful,
he said Trump would win,
and I didn't want to believe
him.

When did Us become a We
and then a kinda,
and then space between the
sheets?
Why didn't I want to be closer
to you?
Why did you see things so much
clearer,
but couldn't notice
the space became you against
I?

You in your high fancy twin
bed,
and me on this lumpy air
mattress,
Trump will win.
And I'm resigned to that fate.

My Body is a Ghost

I have forgotten what touch
feels like,
too certain did I see your
face.
The coolness to the touch,
the essence of who I am,
through you.

Did you not think I would make
it out alive?
The piercing of your soul that
penetrates
through the neither regions of
my legs,
Oh, Hell, not worthy of your
hate.

Finding you not here,
I face my trouble alone.
I'm done with the lies,
The missing signs.

I find myself repeating
the bedroom we lay in,
the cool AC on my body,
the sweat that lays between
us.

The words “I Love You” should
mean something.
You were not the first I said
it to.
Do you really believe it?
Or are you just high?

The ache I feel
must be the spirit beyond.
Fleeting is the wind,
as I bend nature for you.

Last ditch attempts,
make me smile.
Do you really care?
Or is it all a lie?

Why did you give me those jade
beads?
Were you just trying to give
away,
the things you once loved?
Was I a filler in your
in-between
part of an all-consuming,
never-ending
round of girls?
Were you just going through
the motions?
Playing out your what-ifs
before
settling down?

My ghost is on reruns.
The soul keeps going back to
that moment,
the moment with you,
the moment we were tangled up
in the spirit,
the high we felt for each
other,
the intoxication of lust at
its highest.

Your love was fake.
Even I could see through it.
You needed someone to hold
your hand
so you could wake up.

It makes no difference what
you are now.
Your imprint on my body will
never leave.
The damage is done.

My memories will fade,
But the touch of you
won't.

Replacements are Overrated

You're a poor replacement,
Where is the closeness?
The sexual tension as we sit,
in these cold leather seats,
where's the know-how?

I sit and see the pretty
sights and sounds,
I talked of you today,
did you hear me calling?
My poor replacement doesn't
get it like you did.
Why am I trying to make him
into you?

He's a buffer between what I
want,
and can't have.
I miss the sexual tension,
the fuckability, and the
trust,
the knowing we are in this
together,
the miles you drove to meet
me.

He’s a poor replacement for
you.
I miss the warmth, the close
embraces,
the jokes, the toothy grin,
the casual, sensual nature of
it all,

The knowing we weren’t meant
to be,
and knowing no replacement
will ever be good enough.

Mere Misses

Just a mere miss,
miss connection to a life.
Life is a strange thing, a
beautiful one,
beautiful is the taste of
coffee,
coffee refuels the brain
connectors.
Connectors by near misses,
misses are sometimes left
unsaid.

Unsaid words format my stories
left open.
Open up your mouth and let the
words speak,
speak loudly, boldly with your
stories.
Stories are for people who
take adventures,
adventures require trust in
the driver.

Driver who steered past the
cause,
cause meet effect.
Effect meet a small world,
World: you're not alone.

Confession

I did it to love you more,
to show you your worth more,
because I was tired,
tired of your self doubt,
your second guessing,
Your bullshit and values.

Don't you know yourself
better?
Don't you know you're only
like this?
I wanted a love I couldn't
ruin.

Which is why I never said it,
I buried it away,
Forgotten in an old tomb,
Never to be found.

But somehow,
the plate was clean now,
the love came out anyway.

This information got out,
They say love is through
action,
Well, I acted and didn't
think,
I love you.

True Love

Is love an obligation?
Did I move here only to be
stuck?
In a city of broken angels?
Did I choose this life for
five years on purpose?
Should I have stayed in the
South,
or tried Atlanta instead?
Did it even matter,
or would it have been the
same,
merry go round?
The dizzing cycle.

For true love, anything goes.
If you say *jump*,
I question how *high*.
I was blinded by the truth,
Love painted over,
What never could be.
I thought I came here to get
ahead,
But really, I was chasing you.

It's that love I had for you
in your final days,
The friendship I discovered in
your older years,
The love I saw between the two
of you.

You showed me what it meant,
How I was supposed to be,
That selfless love,
That final moment of action,
Of holding your hand and
saying goodbye.

Los Angeles was an obligation,
But seeing you wasn't.

Goodbye, true love.
Goodbye to the endless
adventures,
forever breakfast dates,
To stories of Chicago and
baking,
True love teaches you life,
It shows you what's important,
People are more important
than,
trivial dreams.

Choose life.
Not work.
True love matters.
Even if it lasts,
only a short time.

Sleeping While Standing

The story of resistance,
Tells a long tale,
They told me I should have
given up,
that I wasn't built to hold
this.
They wondered why I didn't
break,
Why I didn't vanish into a
ward,
and surrender to a deep sleep.

When you lose your best friend
to death,
how do you cope?
You wash hope over the heart
like a thin veil,
The tears you push away that
swim in a river of porridge.
I was sleeping while standing,
on the bridge,
wondering which way to go.

Days of sitting in darkness,
I wondered -
How could death rob the
robber?
What all did you steal?
My heart,
My love,
the security of everything I
knew.

I drown my tears in sorrow and
hate.
You don't know me.
You're asleep at the wheel.

I watch the moments go by,
Unfeeling as I sit,
With cooling coffee in my
hand,
While you drop off your
children at school,
I sit unfeeling,
Family is hazy as it passes me
by,
The love for them freezes in
isolation.

I put up walls so it hurts
less,
If I don’t miss them,
I’m fine.
Two thousand miles doesn’t
mean much on paper,
And less around holidays.
Just don’t look at the open
door.
Don’t count the lost
traditions that
Made up a life for twenty-five
years.
What do you do on year
twenty-six?

I am a robot
with no programmable parts.

Broken walls are never meant
to stay.
Every time I thought I was
done.
New tears fell,
Hard topics circling in my
brain.
With minutes counted.
Tick tock
I can’t keep playing this
game,
My heart is fragile,
aching to be mended.
Walls aren’t meant to be this
strong.
I want to feel again.

I’ve lost what I loved most.
Still I go on,
Asleep at the wheel,
still driving.
Don’t look now.

Imposter Syndrome

The shadow breaks and cracks,
through the door I swear I saw
my reflection,
in the puddle of old wood, and
then hanging
on the jagged, broken glass on
the wall.

A deep cloud falls on me,
and all I see is black smoke,
cursing at me and finding ways
to say:
You don't belong here.

On stage I'm in the spotlight,
alone on the empty wood.
the stands, they sit vacant.
And I awake but emotionless.

Who's that performing there?
It can't be me there?
Who's that typing those words?
It must be another.

The imposter will always
snicker.
He lies to you at night and
tells you:
You're not good enough.

You can’t make it.
You won’t win.
So give up now.

But Imposter who are you?
That’s not me.
I am who I say I will be.
Not the version you imagine.
You are not the ideal.

Get out. Imposter.
Out of my head.
I’m the leader of my words and
the pen to my soul.

Pierce the Shadowland

In that Shadowland of
darkness,
I am trapped inside.
Lock the key, because I am not
leaving.

These ever-moving, shaking,
revolting thoughts
won't leave. It's there
spiraling out of control.
Except, wait–you liked this
place.
You chose this place,
Because it mattered.

Your values were believed.
You made a plan to believe in
this job,
These people you love.
This job is exhausting and
challenging.

Every day you're pushed to a
new mountain to achieve,
Is it worth the energy?
Every time you push too hard,
you have negative energy.

The next day is dawn.
I must still be in the hot
sun.
This heat will last all day.
I’m not going to win.

Until sleep takes over your
soul,
and there’s release.

The Shadowland plays and
creeps out.
It loves to play and prey on
the tired souls.
When you work for no glory or
fame,
It can steal your joy.

Pierce through the light of
the Shadowland,
by finding the crack you
didn’t know was there,
Bring donuts and see the light
at the long, bright tunnel.

You can survive this.
Maybe.
Or you can:
Quit.

Part Three

3000 Miles In The Bag

The Street

My ex lived in the white
apartment,
for the longest time,
I couldn't go on this street,
this street brought up missed
memories I
Thought I needed,
but I realized I didn't.

God told me for two years to
go to a church,
on this street.
It's funny how this entity,
The Creator,
was right.
This street gave me community,
residence,
and security.

And then one day I left.
It all behind.
this life, these friends,
the people I thought I always
needed,
Were they just place holders?
Did I sow deep enough bonds to
get me through the long night?
Will they still remember me
when I'm gone?

Your Fake Community

I think I'll stay awhile here,
I feel safe here, surrounded
by all of you,
You who stand next to me in
the row,
The quiet, determined you.

You who I think,
I'm close to.
Temporary holding power.
It's all an illusion.

Putting on my best authentic
self.
Raise the hands,
Sing the songs, And don't cry.
Don't let them in, they are
temporary.

Bro, Bro, Bro, Bro, Girl,
Girl, Girl,
Coffee date lady friend?
I'm not like you,
I'm not the same as you.

Oh dear, what have we done?
Don't feel that way.
Don't bring that up.
We are all family here aren't we?
We totally accept you.
We are all family here.

But it's high school all over again,
And I'm at the party for one table.

That new experience,
The feeling of not knowing,
Everyone staring at you,
Until in the crowd,
You see one face,
You know.

There's your community.
Table for one.

LA to OC

Down the 405 I pass,
that palace that looks like
a Taj Mahal
but in the middle of,
The City of Industry.

Past all the tire stores,
trees growing through the
concrete jungle,
and even further pass to
Orange County.
The second you get there.
it seems cleaner,
wider,
less cluttered.
How can a few miles make all
the difference?

The drive, like my head,
cleared the stress.
That stretch of highway
sheds my old skin
into the new.

Blue waters of Huntington,
Big Lots,
a four-square church hidden by
palm trees,
fields, Disneyland,
tourists smiling fill the
streets,
gives me the pleasure of
pretending,
I belong here,
even if I’m visiting,
biding my time,
until I must go back.
Do I have to go back?

Waves

Blow in through the caverns,
the rush of waves below,
the wind guides me forward,
that I know it will push me,
for always I've known my
place,
at the beach I'm home,
go in with the tide,
go out with the detritus,
the rushing of water foam,
fuming, fumbling, fuzing
together.
This is the sound I came for,
waves on the immovable rock.
Here is where the push and
pull stop.

SMUGGLERS COVE

Smuggler's Cove

Up a hill
and through some brush,
you could hear the wind
whispering,
It's a cool shimmer and glow.

The path darts right and left,
Some lead to elsewhere.
I wonder, where is that
elsewhere in my mind?

Loving this, but not the pain.
The letting go,
the knowing.

This might be the last CA
adventure,
for a long time.
It makes it sweeter to know,
It's time spent with good
friends,
skipping rocks along the
shore,
Taking long catnaps and
sunbathing.

For screaming ravens who
cannot settle scores,
a beautiful noise, unlike the
arguments
behind closed doors.

Going the extra distance
is worth the magic of a
beautiful beach.
The treasure lies in the rich
vastness
Of our mind and full hearts.

So now I can go,
quietly, and hear the tunes
of nature's beating language
penetrate my soul.

Channel Islands

Let's get away,
away from it all,
away from cell phones,
Instagram and Flo,
away from the noise,
the pollution,
the rise in temperatures.

To the wilderness,
where foxes live,
where only park rangers
reside.
where you can only get to
by boat and foot.

Where fuzzy, brown and tan
super bugs crawl,
where yellow striped with
black bees buzz,
where ravens, not crows, have
marital disputes
on your picnic table.

Go on, get away from the
noise,
oh wait.
I forgot.
The world is never quiet.
From the sea's low sigh,
to the sky's high hum,
the ambient world is always
present.

A Raven’s Quarrel

Pursuer: What’s that, dear?
Pursuer: What’s that you say?
Pursuer: Dear, please accept
my sock as a representation
Of our love.

Distracted One: What love? Let
me watch that water sea thing.
Pursuer: Oh, dear, please,
What must I do to prove my
love to you?

Distracted One: Hun, this rock
is the most tan. Look, will
you.
Pursuer: Oh, dear, my beak,
I can’t grab this white holy
round thing.
Pursuer: Oh, dear, stop walk-
ing away. I love you!

Distracted One: Hun, come
look. I think I see a large
orange fish floating in the
water.
Pursuer: Oh, dear. Please look
my way! I found a, Crumpled up
piece of Lunchables wrapper
for you. Do you like it?

Distracted One: Hun, isn't it a beautiful day to fly?
Pursuer: Oh, dear! Why she flew away from me.
Pursuer: I must chase after her.

It’s my Turn to Talk

Fumbling, mumbling, grumbling,
shouting,
rude doesn’t begin to define
my anger,
dinner prep and being a
superstar,
I see: parents acting like
children,
Campsite drama can kill a
moment.

Noise. A tentative offering.
It’s all fucked up.

And now, it’s father’s turn to
mansplain to you,
“We worked all year to sell
cookies,
They are eleven and deserve to
be princesses.”

They, at the United Ignoramus
Front,
personally welcome you
to the loudest place on the
island.
admittance is only for your
patients
and tolerance for loud,
bloody, murder screams.

I don’t think you deserve our
peace offering,
so please, try to smile and be
happy campers.

Bitter Wind and Frigid New England

San Gabriel mountains are green,
like the hope of something better.
The blue sky perches up to the sun, hot,
oh so hot,
I'm melting.

But the Santa Ana's are here,
blustery, blowing through the brush.
Blowing intently through my skin.
Oh! Oh! Oh! Whew! Look! A breeze!
Fuck. The hills. The trees.

Fire, fire everywhere I turn.
It's crossing over the 210.
Run. Run east, keep going.
The fire won't get me when I'm East.

The North, I'm safe,
from the bitter wind from the West,
with the frigid God forsaken cold.
Ice cuts of pain. Slicing through
my bones. My brittle bones break.
My spirit goes,
So does the sun down for the day.

Blow through, nor'easter.
I can stand you.
The fire won't get me here.
We are safe now.
The wind can't carry that black smoke
my way.

Safe fire, stay put.
Bring the rain.
Pour over and shower my sins,
my thoughts in the ashes of
my abandoned memoirs.

Lost to fate and indecision.
I lost you, fire, but I gained
the wind.

Dreams of Dust and Shadows

If you could see me now,
The bright lights of New York.
Just kidding, that's the start
of a song.

What I feel is the distance
between
what I want and what I feel I
can't achieve.
Is it even possible to get
what you want anymore?
In the age of everything
changing.

Does it matter to exist?
Does it matter to keep trying?
Or will the robots take over,
silencing anything with
feeling?

Will I get that deal or make
my mark?
At the end of the day, will
you remember me?
Am I just ash in the dust?

Ode to 2016

To you I honor you,
For you are like a flower
slowly wilting in misty
shadow.
The year for envy, love,
misogyny and triumph,
The You in all Yous,
You're more perfect than
Helvetica.

To go forward you must go
backwards.
Misadventures, dead ends,
elections and malfunctions,
Tests, GRE, patients, waiting,
and Whole Foods,
Long afternoons in a lazy
summer heat,
Beauty wrapped up in wine
hazed memories,

Vows, romance, couples,
loneliness,
Relationships happen when
you're not looking,
Stop looking for a
relationship,
Shakespeare and the death of
You,
Missing hands, and one man's
love,
Fierce powerful Zen spirit,

Honesty, words, time, space,
endings,
Stupid mistakes, and missed
opportunities,
New friendships, renewed
faith, that little white
church,
Crushes, flings and misguided
nights out,
Searching for the truth,
While standing on a mountain
overlooking,
Hobbits, farms and a best
friend,

Long plane rides, inner self,
fear, and reconciliation,
New beginnings fall upon the
summer air,
Sweet, sweaty couches full
of maracas and teakettles on
fire,
Peppermint, Alpine, fires and
raindrops,
Dedication to honoring those
before you,

Road trips, unexpected ideas
and abandoned waterparks,
Hiking, treetops, wisdom tree,
deep conversations,
9am, coffee, bibles, and
beautiful prayers,
Juarez, Alvin, Trolls and
singing will never go out of
style,
Indie movies, funny
coincidences and weird stop
motion sex scenes,
White winter hymnal, red foxes
and Christmas.

To you 2016 I will remember
thee,
You were full of life, love
and thousands of stories that
will never get written down.

An Ode To 2017

To cold nights,
To warm summers,
To writing pages in a hotel
room,
To fuzzy pineapple slippers
and empty bars alone,
To the solace of quiet and
contemplative thoughts,
To Phoenix, a happy accident,
and Harry Potter.

To learning to love alone,
And knowing the difference
between that and everything
else.
To more monthly hits and
greater oceans leaped,
To many weekends indoors
sitting on the couch,
To essays, classes and no
social life.

To the little white church and
new kinds of family,
To revelations, honest prayer
and damn commitment,
To fear, and misdirection, and
all that is apart of the life,
kid.

To the little white church and
new kinds of family,
To revelations, honest prayer
and damn commitment,
To fear, and misdirection, and
all that is apart of the life,
kid.

To sweat-stained couches,
laundromats for the last time
this year,
To car parks and creepy
alleys,
To FaceTime chats,
To phones being stuck in
pockets and new family h
istories,
To walking around
neighborhoods and a movie
buddy,
To boba, sushi and downtown LA
ramen,
To food trucks, finally good
beer, and a group of friends,
To monthly writer meetings and
moving on.

To packing my life up in
boxes,
To never wanting to leave this
hot bed,
To staring up at the ceiling,
while my friends pack my life
away,
To mimosa's and wine in red
solo cups,
To 3000 plus miles in the bag,
To four weeks that forever
changed my life,
To taking a chance and never
looking back.

For living my best life,
To new friends who are
seriously the smartest people
on a level I'll never
understand,
To old friends becoming new
again and realizing we are
just picking up where we left
off,
To Zunizi's, the Fleet Foxes,
my girl who got me through the
last two years of my life.

To getting caught in the rain,
and seeing snow for the first
time,
To going down sideways
streets,
To not being able to pronounce
a goddamn city name.
To Thanksgivings that are too
good for words,
To a Black Friday that will
never be forgotten,
To a tiny Thai restaurant that
I felt like I spent hours in.

To laughing out loud for what
seemed like ever,
To finding the best wine in
the world because you let me
take a chance,
To letting the end of one
thing be the beginning of
something else.
To gaining three new sisters
that I never asked for,
But always had wanted.
To my first new years kiss and
dancing like I've never danced
before.

To you 2017.
It’s time I move on.
Don’t look back.
It only gets better from here.

Ode to 2018

2018 in all its glory. An Ode
to YOU.
Let's give it up for all the
players,
In life we call friends,
Family,
Co-workers.
The ones who work and live on
passion in their tiny
apartments,
Making music until the morning
light,
Dancing up all night in secret
clubs and music you've never
heard before,
To the midnight rushes and
sushi dates at 7.

All fair in love in war.
To giving love one last shot
and getting stomped in the
heart
On the way to work
Over Snapchat.

To winter winds, and
Nor'Easters that won't quit,
To pour overs and breakfast
tacos,
To the mountains of Asheville
and the Blue Ridge Parkway.
To homemade dumplings and
friendship in snow piles,
To funny squished noses on
dogs and diners that hark back
to
College,
To all the holidays that
seemed broken,
To which I say now are mended.
People make the moment, not
the technology.

To dreams finally taking
flight,
And long days ahead,
To sleepless coughing nights,
And data meetings that just
don’t seem right,
Oh what a year,
Of super highs that even Paul
Revere would smile at,
TO the lowest of lows and
never-ending fights,
Where the beautiful and the
damned slept tonight,
Finding the way through this
year was like combing hair in
an ice storm,
It just never happened.
Who even goes out in an ice
storm?

To unexpected deaths that seem
like a laundry list of
sadness,
To the love of life, love and
loss published in a small
book,
A quiet place for one reader
and the peace of mind to
another,
Poetry takes on a new
dimension as it grows and
intertwines,
With the burnt taste of
mosquitoes and the able-bodied
lambs.

Thank you, 2018.
Let's remember you fondly of
the best and worst of us.
Moved on.
Without you.
Forgot you.
Ate you like a delicious taco
loves ramen.

Jennifer Kain is a writer and filmmaker. You can find more of her work at jenniferkain.me and on Instagram: jenkainwrites

www.ingramcontent.com/pod-product-compliance
Lightning Source LLC
LaVergne TN
LVHW010902110826
845149LV00005B/1443

* 9 7 9 8 9 9 4 4 3 4 8 4 0 *